prologue:

hi friends – so happy you have chosen to read this poetry book. Now I know no one really reads a prologue but I figured I would write one to let you in on how this book came to be. I was in between jobs, I am a nurse, and I have always loved poetry. I started writing little poems in my notes section on my phone and well it seems I now have a book. These poems are little bits of my life and what I have experienced. I wanted to share them with you in hopes that it may resonate with your soul and make you think. I want to say now thank you so much for taking the time to read this little book of mine. lots of love – Ashley.

I'm a sunflower baby
I grow in different shapes
Different directions
A mellow yellow that no one understands

can be like a peony
nd blush pink
ut I can also be like a rose
nd grow thorns

Why do people think
They can treat you like garbage
When all you try to do
Is help them

ot everyone understands
ow multifaceted I am

Who do you think you are?
Leaving these scars
These scars don't define me
But they show me where I've been
Who's hurt me
And then I remember without these
I wouldn't be me

hy do men think it's ok to play
ith your heartstrings and then rip your heart out afterwards?

Good girls are prudes
Bad girls are sluts
What the fuck enough with the labels

ou on your throne thinking you're the king
Well honey I've got news for you
ou're nothing but an asshole

Society is fucked
Why do we care if she is dating him or her?
Why do we care if he or she is a virgin?
Why do we care if they've gained weight?
Let's look into the souls of people
That's where the real beauty lies
We are all too caught up on self-image
Society is fucked

e happy with you
ind things you love
elf-love isn't selfish
ove yourself first
nd everything else will fall into place

My dear,
It's ok to cry
But just remember once you're done
But some lipstick on
And remember who you are
A true badass

Women truly amaze me
How can someone be so strong
so empowering
so brilliant
so breathtaking
I'm at a loss for words
And that's bad for a poet

I've seen death
I've seen people take their last breath
It's quite peaceful actually
To know that there's something more powerful than us out there
Faith is a must in a world like this

impress me with your intellect
tell me something spiritual
let me see your soul

"What's wrong with me
Am I not good enough"
These are the things I used to think
When men didn't like me
Well maybe it's not meant to be
Did you ever think of that?
Maybe God has a different path
We are all ticking on different clocks
Be patient my love

My love,
When I find you
I'll know because I'll feel whole,
open, brave, and honest

Maybe the one you were searching for was yourself all along. You are magnificent.

ll you need in this life of sin
a good bottle of gin

I once had a boy tell me I didn't know what Love was because I've never been in a serious relationship
At first I got hurt by this remark
Then I realized how shallow this boy was
How could he possibly know how I've ever felt
I know what Love is
I've seen it with my own eyes
I've watched families together in the hospital, I've watched families stay with their loved ones while they pass away
I've seen love in my parents
I've seen love in my friendships
I've seen love between my siblings and I
Love isn't stuck to one type of relationship Love is in all things
Then I realized how sorry I felt for this boy who truly didn't know what Love was.

et's radiate love
ove is the answer to everything
we really think about it
verything comes down to love

Everyone tells me 'just be happy'
Why do I always have to be fucking happy.

but darling
you're a lion
Why do you give a shit about these sheep

You're a fucking wildflower baby
No one can hold you down
So bloom baby bloom

o you ever just not speak because you're worried people won't understand
hat you're trying to say

People with no anxiety don't understand people with anxiety
Also how do you not have anxiety in a world like this

ou ever wake up shaking
nsure what's going on
ou breathe and breathe and that doesn't work
nd then you pop that happy pill
nd it all goes away?
me.

Respect is huge in days like these
Respect yourself most of all
People will try to take advantage of your good nature
You deserve the best
Don't let anyone tell you otherwise

Open up your heart
You could find love
Or heartbreak
But isn't it better to try than to keep those walls up?
The walls are fucking heavy.

People always say I have this mysterious vibe
They can't really understand me
I look at them and think no one is one emotion, thought, concept
So don't put me in a box

eople often tell me I am intimidating
ut that just confuses me because I am a welcoming and warm person
ure I am quiet at first
ut maybe you just do not want to put the effort into knowing me
ounds like a you problem

I fall in love
And I cry and cry
Because I know it's not forever

Trust is really hard
When those you fall for
Always seem to leave you

Boys nowadays
All they want to do is take off your clothes
They do not really want to get to know your mind
Do not let them manipulate your kind soul
You are so much more than your skin and bones
You deserve someone to sweep you off your feet
With their kind words and heart
Messaging you saying they want to see you naked is not a compliment
That's just gross. You are worth so much more. Do not forget that.

hat boy is not that great
e is paper
e is fake
e only wants one thing
o not let him get what he wants
ou are strong
ou need a man who will take you out and treat you right.

Why do guys think its ok to slide into your dm's
"you're hot"
                Dude, I know but I am so much more

                                        So bye

hose lips
he things I would do to just kiss them once more

I am not sure what I need
All I know is it is something more
Something magnificent

ishing, waiting, wanting more
will kill you
ccept you for you
ccept what you have for now
he universe will give you the rest

Honey, some people do not deserve your kindness
Do not feel bad for not giving them what they want
After all, it is your life
You get what YOU want.

What happened to romance
asking a girl out for dinner
pulling out her chair and pushing it in
is this all gone
or was it just in the movies and I am just being naïve
hope not.

Comparing yourself to others is poisonous
We are all beautiful in our own ways
Radiate confidence and self-love
And the universe will give you that back

The feeling you have when you're under water
You feel tranquil, calm, weightless
I want to feel that
With you.

I get too nervous to say what is on my mind
I am worried people will not like me for me
But then I remember the queen that I am
And you should too.

he keeps trying to tear that wall down
but she keeps finding reasons to stack it with bricks
There's a lot of scenarios where she can keep stacking bricks
but there are so many more reasons to be open and unguarded
That's when love comes in

They keep pulling at her
In different directions
But she stands tall and knows which way she should go

The fear of failure should not be a motivator
Think about how many times you have succeeded
Failure is just a speed bump on the way to success
Every success has a failure
Keep failing, you'll get there

You feel so close to me
Yet you are so distant
I cannot tell what you want
I'm not a mind reader
But I'm hoping you don't leave

ıe's not up for the game you're playing
ıe knows that you'll leave in the end
ɔ she stops it before you can
ıe's no fool

There are times when she has to say no
She's growing stronger each day
She realizes that loving herself is the best way to get through this life

he power of the waves crashing
what I feel when I am with you

The steel blue eyes make me weak
I look into them and think
There's nothing we cannot do together

ey babe you got a voice of angel
s smooth as caramel
ng me to sleep in your arms

I notice you
Do you notice me?
I wish you could look at me
The way you look at her

someday, some way
i will find the love of my life
God does not rush life
so why should you

Anxiety is caused by society
Society makes us think we are not good enough
We do not belong
We have weird habits
Weird is good, weird is fun
Do not be afraid to be yourself
There is only one you

you are like a strong wind
omph, ripping up the roots of giant oak trees
you are unstoppable
believe in yourself
if you do not believe in yourself, no one will

I think sometimes we meet someone
Who is not on the same spiritual path
And that's ok
Everyone is on a different path in this life
We cannot change that
God has a plan for everyone
We need to be patient and kind to everyone
Who knows what others are going through
All we can do as people is love on another
We all have our faults
No one is perfect
Perfectly imperfect

o we really all have one person for the rest of our lives
 soulmate seems almost impossible
ut I guess that is what makes it all worth it
 the end you are with someone who you could never replace
hat's why it is so rare and so precious
 you find that then you better savior that forever
o not give up on it
eep loving

That smile on your face kills me
Those dimples
Those lips
The way your eyes light up when you see me
That's what I love about you

these pills do not help me
i need to remember the cure is inside me
i will not let this control me
it does not define me
it will not have me
i will never give up this fight

Mental health is one of those things
If you are mentally healthy you live longer
Happiness is the cure to all things
Even if you die young, but were happy with the life you lived
You cannot be mad

beauty comes from the inside
if you are ugly on the inside
you are ugly on the outside
never let a horrible person make you feel bad
they are not worth your time or thoughts
they are just too sad to feel anything

You are so good looking
It actually hurts
How can someone be such a charmer
It is unnerving how I feel about you
You make me so happy

I find myself thinking a lot about how I am not "her"
I am not as pretty, as smart, as charming
Then I realize I do not even know "her"
She is a figure of my imagination
How can I compare myself to someone I do not know
I am strong, educated, empowered and witty
I need to remember to love myself
Be confident in the You that you created

What if they judge me for writing these words
What if they do not like these poems
I am sure everyone has felt the same way about their compassions
If they are going to be tormented for writing or saying what they feel
It is what you feel
No one has the right to tell you what you feel
These are your emotions and they belong to you
You do not have to justify yourself to anyone

is like I am in a dream with you
this is a dream please do not wake me
want to be with you like this forever
y minds dream is sometimes better than reality

I feel so stuck
What am I supposed to do with my life
What is my purpose
Are we supposed to know the answer
How do we get through this reality
When sometimes it is actual Hell
I guess that is why God made a Heaven
So once we are done here we can finally be in paradise
Find the ultimate happiness and truth

when you finally get what you want
it is ok to feel happy for yourself
to be proud
congratulate yourself
that does not make you selfish or conceited
it is ok to pat yourself on the back
you deserve it

Choose you
Choose love
Choose happiness

an you not see how much I love you
look into your eyes and it is like I have entered another world
eep taking me places that I do not know
want to learn everything in your mind
enjoy our time
cannot wait to keep learning and loving
tay with me

Keep growing
Keep learning
Keep being

his whiskey tastes as bitter as your soul
ot everyone likes every type of alcohol
ome things have a very particular taste

You are as smooth as this green tea shot
Sweet as the peach schnapps
With a little kick of Jameson Irish whiskey
Keeping me on my toes
I like that

Cancer attacks the whole body
Once the mind is gone, there is nothing left
The mind is everything
Without this we have no soul
We are no longer there
Cherish your experience on this earth
Not everyone gets so much time

Those brown eyes
Just like milk chocolate
Sweet and innocent
With gold flecks
Not as harsh as dark chocolate
But still have some mystery

My friends do not understand
What it feels like to not be able to go out to social gatherings
Without feeling out of place
Sometimes I go to the bathroom just to hide from people
God, I love anxiety

It must be really nice to sleep through the night
Without having thoughts running through your mind
I can never turn off my mind
Too many scenarios to think about
Half of the time I know these situations would never happen
But my brain does not get that I guess

it bad to say that you bore me
need someone that I can connect with spiritually
someone who understands me so much so that I do not have to explain
yself
am too multifaceted for a one faceted person

I just want a fairytale love affair
One where I cannot believe this is my life
Someone who can read and understand my inner thoughts
Treats me kindly and with respect
Is that too much to ask?

eople say I have "too high of standards"
itch I will never settle
ot when it comes to something as precious as Love

Let's get lost
Does not matter where we are
I could easily just get lost in those eyes
Let's go somewhere extravagant
I have always dreamed of the islands of Greece

you are stuck on my mind
like a drug addict seeking for their heroin
Why don't you leave me alone
I do not want you anymore

"Hey girl you up"
Nah bro I am not
Especially not for you

self-respect and self-love are the most powerful things anyone can have
without these things we cannot set boundaries
we become pushovers
sometimes we forget we can say "no"
you are not going to disappoint them
do not worry they will move onto their next girl
i just hope she has as much self-respect as I do
we all deserve respect – for ourselves and for others

Sometimes I think no one understands me
That scares the shit out of me
I am waiting for that connection
I need to feel loved and be loved
Maybe I am just needy

There is a beauty about being alone
You learn about yourself each day
That you like and do not like
This way you know what to look for in a lover
Not everyone gets to spend time alone and live by themselves
Cherish the time by yourself
You need to learn about you first before you let someone else in

I am afraid to let people into my life
I have seen so many people lose loved ones
Whether it is from death or heartbreak or both
I am just not sure if it is worth it
Then again, I need to remember that life is fleeting
As cheesy as that sounds
We cannot let fear rule out lives

my brain is all over the place
just like these poems
am sorry

You cut me deep
Just like the Grand Canyon
People do not usually have that affect on me
That's when I knew you were different

My heart is racing because of my thoughts
All of a sudden I am in tachycardia
Confused as to why
That's the beautiful thing about a panic attack
It comes out of no where

'I cannot breathe
My throat is closing
Why is this happening to me
Why are you crushing my heart'
These are just the thoughts that I have
When I am having a panic attack
Sounds fun right?

think your kisses may cure whatever is happening inside of me
this tortured self esteem
skewed self-worth
then I remember what my therapist told me
this does not happen from loving someone
this comes from loving yourself

What do you want from me
I need to know that you will be here when I say you are all I want
I have been fucked with too many times
I am not about to get hurt again
Do not tear down my walls just to screw me over

here is a light inside of you
hat is as bright as the sun
o one can cancel out that light except you
eep shining babe

You were uniquely designed by God
Do not destroy that essence of beauty
He put together your ingredients with precision
A variety of spices were used to create you.

No one knows what it is like to be you
Only you know that
It is important to remember to be open with people
This way they can understand you
However, only spill your true self with those you trust
Now, that is the tricky part
Not everyone is worth knowing the real you
Remember you are a prize.

Everyone wants to be happy
So why do we hurt each other
What is the point of spreading negativity
When positivity is so much more beautiful

o not be an asshole
is quite easy

I have been craving you for a while now
I just never knew how to tell you
So I am telling you now
Hope it is not too late

emember to always love yourself first...

Xx Ashley

Made in the USA
Coppell, TX
12 July 2021

58859441R00057